Beginner Guitar Lessons for Kids

Book with Online Video and Audio Access

By
Jay Wamsted

For Online Video & Audio Access, go to this address on the internet:

cvls.com/extras/kidsguitar

Watch & Learn, Inc.

About the Author

Jay Wamsted teaches high school math in southwest Atlanta. He has been playing guitar for over thirty years—sometimes in bands and sometimes alone. He holds a Ph.D. in education from Georgia State University and his published writing can be found both online and in various journals and magazines. In addition to teaching math, he has taught private lessons for both piano and guitar; currently he is working with his own children on these very arrangements. Several of his original piano compositions can be streamed at Amazon Play, Apple Music, Spotify, and elsewhere.

Watch & Learn Products Really Work

Over thirty years ago, Watch & Learn revolutionized instructional music courses by developing well thought out, step-by-step methods. These courses were tested for effectiveness on beginners before publication. These lessons have continued to improve and evolve into the Watch & Learn system that continues to set the standard of music instruction today. This has resulted in sales of more than three million products since 1979.

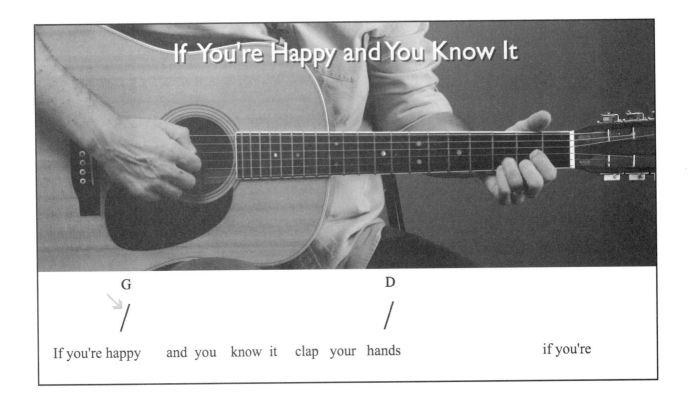

About this Course

This course was designed for elementary school-aged children (5 years and up) with an emphasis on getting the student to play real music as quickly as possible. Our method is unique because of two basic concepts. First, we teach songs that many kids will already know. This avoids the student becoming overwhelmed by learning rhythm notation. Secondly, the chord shapes and strum patterns taught are intentionally very simple. This allows the student to have early success and get interested in playing the guitar without getting overly frustrated and giving up.

In Section 2 of the course, we teach simple songs using easier or partial chord shapes that are suitable for students with smaller hands. For students who are older or have larger hands, we've included the same songs with full chord shapes in Section 3. This allows each student to play the songs using techniques that are size appropriate.

It's important for the student to know that everyone learns at a different speed. Younger children may require more guidance to work through the book. It's also important for adults to remember to encourage the student and be proud of any progress that is made.

Course Material

In addition to this book, you also have access to video instruction that covers all of the songs taught in the book. This is an important tool for helping the student play in time and with proper form.

We've also included access to audio tracks for each song. These can be downloaded and used to practice away from a screen.

cvls.com/extras/kidsguitar

If you ever need any assistance accessing or using these materials, please send an email to sales@cvls.com. The tracks feature piano and guitar by Jay Wamsted. The tracks were recorded by Toby Ruckert at uTOBYa Studio.

Table of Contents

Section 1: Getting Started

Parts of the Guitar 1

The Headstock 2

The Neck 3

The Body 4

Seated Position 5

Right Hand 6

Strumming 7

Tuning the Guitar 8

Left Hand 9-10

The G Chord 11-12

G Chord Song 13

C Chord Song 14

Changing Chords 15

Practice Tips 16

Section 2: The Songs 17

He's Got the Whole World 18-19

Mary Had a Little Lamb 20-21

Wheels On the Bus 22-23

Row, Row, Row Your Boat 24-25

Hush Little Baby 26-27

Rain, Rain, Go Away 28-29

Hokey Pokey.................................30-31

If You're Happy and You Know It........32-33

Itsy Bitsy Spider.................................34-35

John Jacob Jingleheimer Schmidt........36-37

Oh When the Saints 38-39

Twinkle Twinkle Little Star 40-41

Section 3: The Songs with Full Chords 42

G, C, D, & D^7 chords 43

He's Got the Whole World 44-45

Mary Had a Little Lamb 46-47

Wheels On the Bus...........................48-49

Row, Row, Row Your Boat 50-51

Hush Little Baby 52-53

Rain, Rain, Go Away..........................54-55

Hokey Pokey.......................................56-57

If You're Happy and You Know It........58-59

Itsy Bitsy Spider.................................60-61

John Jacob Jingleheimer Schmidt........62-63

Oh When the Saints 64-65

Twinkle Twinkle Little Star 66-67

Common Chords 68-69

Follow-up Products............................70-71

Section 1
Getting Started

For Online Video & Audio Access, go to this address on the internet:

cvls.com/extras/kidsguitar

Parts of the Guitar

There are three main sections of the guitar: the headstock, the neck, and the body. There are small differences between an acoustic guitar and an electric guitar. However, you can use either type of guitar to work through this course.

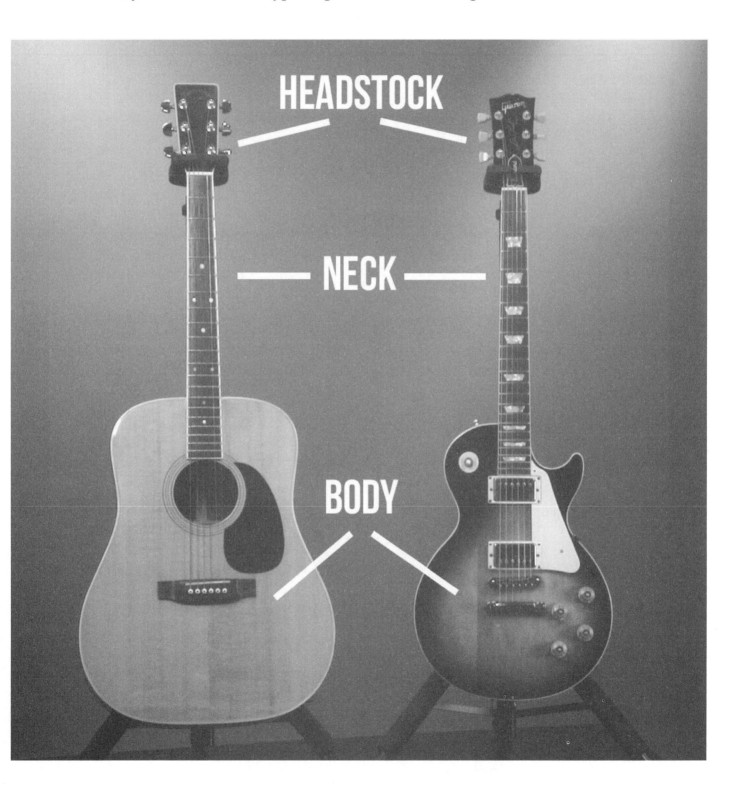

The Headstock

The tuning keys are used to tighten and loosen the strings. This allows you to tune each string to the proper note.

The nut helps hold the strings in place.

When you make the string vibrate with your finger or by striking it with a pick, you create sound.

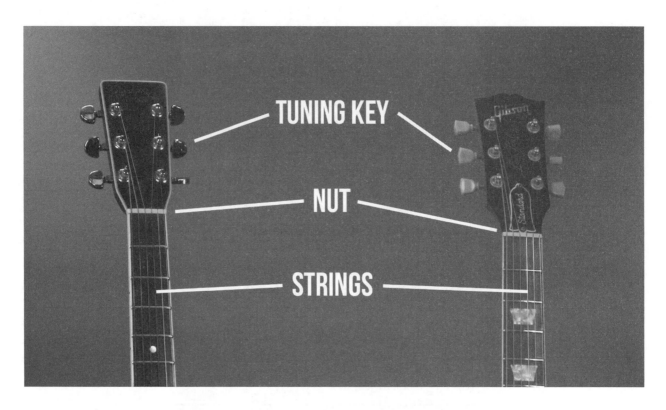

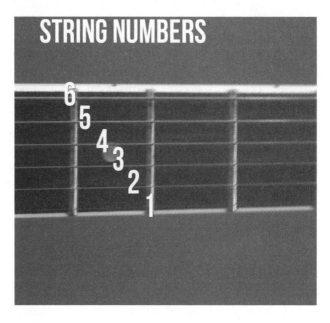

The Neck

The frets are metal bars on the neck of the guitar. When you play a string, and hold the string against a fret, it creates a note.

There are dots or other designs on the neck known as fret markers. These markers allow you to quickly figure out which fret is which.

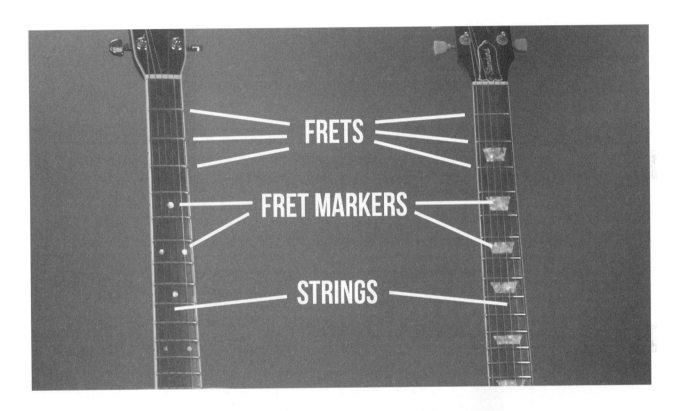

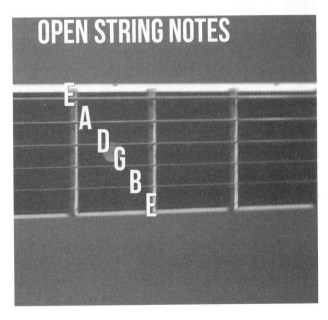

The Body

The sound hole on an acoustic guitar is where the sound of the strings becomes louder. On an electric guitar, the pickups are used to collect the sound and make it louder.

The pick guard does exactly what its name says it does. It protects the wood on your guitar from being damaged by the pick while you play.

The bridge holds the strings in place just like the nut does at the other end of the neck.

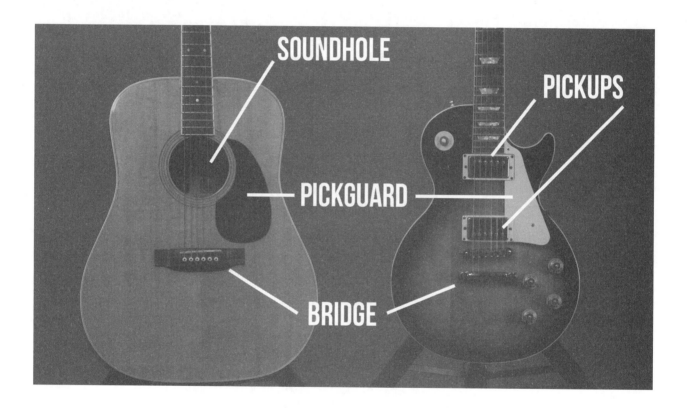

Seated Position

When you first start playing guitar, it's easiest to use a seated position. You want to use a basic and comfortable chair that doesn't have arms on either side. You also want the height of the seat to allow your upper leg to be at an even position with your knee. This provides a good spot to rest your guitar.

Right Hand

The most common way to play a guitar is to use a pick or plectrum. This is typically a triangle shaped piece of plastic that allows you to strike the strings and create a louder volume.

In the beginning, you may want to try using a thin or low gauge pick. They are a little bit easier to play with. You may also find that using a felt ukulele pick is easier to hold and doesn't play too loudly.

Don't have a pick? No problem. You can always use your thumb to strum the strings.

The most common way to hold the pick is between the thumb and index finger. First, you want to curl your index finger. With your left hand, place the pick on top of your index finger, then place your thumb on top of the pick with enough force to hold it in place.

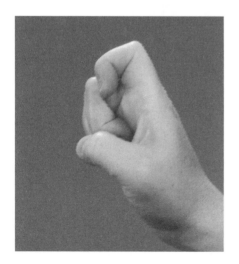  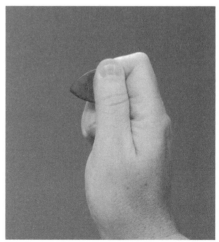

Strumming

You will use the pick to brush over the strings. When we play a few strings at the same time, we call it strumming.

Using your elbow to move your arm, try to strum the strings while you move your arm down. On you way back up, don't play any strings.

Now try to play each string one at a time starting from the string closest to the ceiling. This is called the 6th string and plays the note E, the 5th string is the note A, 4th string is a D, 3rd string is a G, 2nd string is a B, and the 1st is another E.

Did your strings sound different than mine? It might be because your guitar is out of tune. Your guitar is probably made of wood, has metal strings, and has the tuning pegs, nuts, and bridge holding everything in place. Unfortunately, these different parts get bigger and smaller and move around over time or just because the temperature changes. When this happens, we have to make sure our strings are playing those notes (E, A, D, G, B, E) correctly. This process is called tuning.

Tuning the Guitar

The most common way to tune your guitar is with either an electronic tuner or a tuning app. Luckily, most of these work the same way. If you play the 3rd string (G), you may see a G show up on the screen. If the note your string is playing is too low or flat, you might see an F or F♯. You will need to tighten your string a little until you see the G show up in the middle. If the note played by your 3rd string is too high, you may see A♭ or A. This means you need to loosen your string a little.

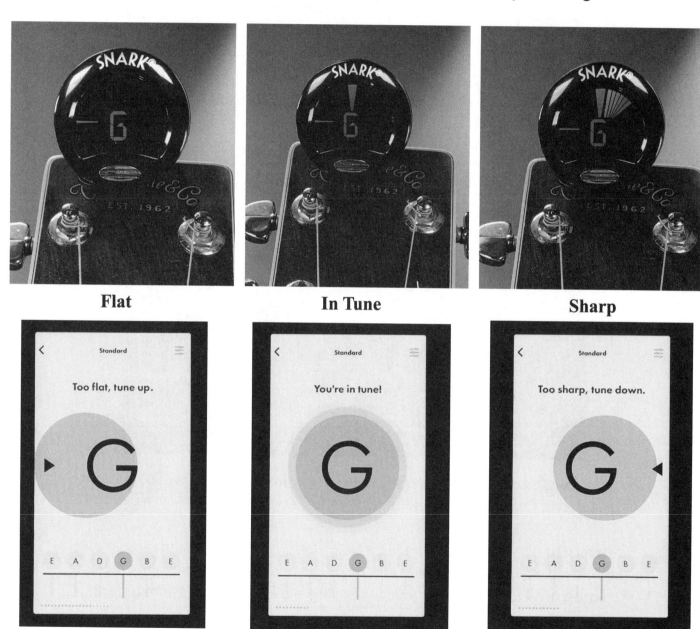

| Flat | In Tune | Sharp |

We then need to repeat this process for all six strings (E, A, D, G, B, E) until they are playing the correct note. It's important that you tune your guitar at the start of each practice session. Playing an out of tune guitar is like baking a cake with the wrong ingredients. No matter how hard you try, it won't end up tasting very good. Even famous guitarists would sound bad if they play out of tune guitars.

Left Hand

We can use our left hand to make the guitar play lots of different notes. Let's look at how that works.

We start by putting our left hand thumb on the back of the guitar neck. Most guitarists put their thumb in the middle of the curve of the neck. If you have a longer thumb, you may place it higher, and if your hand is smaller, you may need to place it lower.

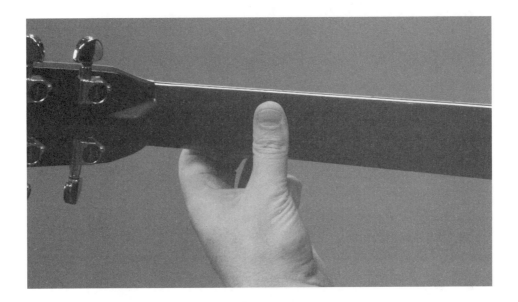

Your thumb will also be on the opposite side of the neck from the 2nd or 3rd fret for most of this course. To make a note, the left hand fingers push the strings against the neck.

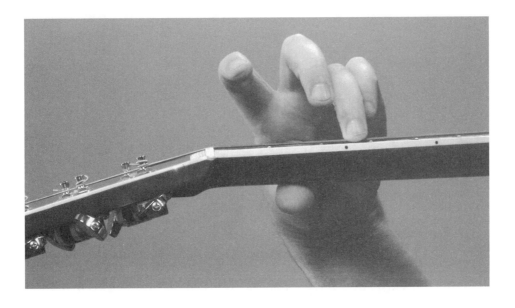

On the 1st string, we're going to place our left ring finger just behind the third fret. You don't want to be directly on top of the fret, and you don't want to be too far behind. You're pushing down just below the fret. If you push too hard, your finger will get too tired. If you push too light, you will hear a buzzing sound. So try to push just enough to hear a clear note.

Correct

Too far from fret

Too close to fret

With a pick in your right hand, try playing the first string, while your left ring finger pushes down from just behind the third fret. This note is a G.

The G Chord

When we play several notes at the same time, it's called a chord. Let's learn our first chord.

When you learn chords, you'll be told how to play them by using a chord diagram. It looks like the neck of the guitar has been rotated up-right and you're looking directly at it.

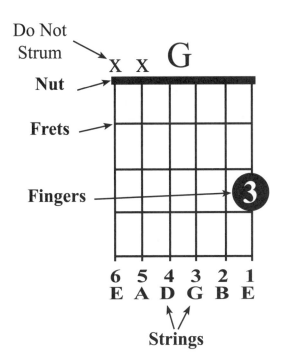

This is our first chord, G. The diagram shows you which frets and strings to place your fingers on. Our left hand is numbered 1 2 3 4. So the number 3 shows us that we're putting our ring finger on the 3rd fret of the 1st string. The x's at the top mean that we don't strum the 6th and 5th strings for this chord.

The fingers are numbered as in the diagram to the right.

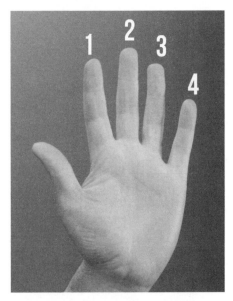

11

The Strum

With our right hand, we're going to play strings 4,3,2, and 1 at the same time with a strum.

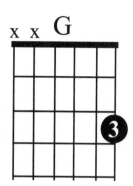

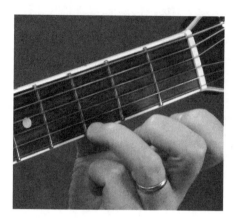

Now, let's play the G chord. Brush over the strings with your pick from the 4th string down towards the floor. Play the strum so that it sounds like all of the strings are being played at the same time. If you can hear each individual string as you strum down, then you're playing it too slowly.

Count out loud, 1 2 3 4. Try to strum down each time you say a number. When we strum down, you will see the following symbol in our music (/).

Chord ➝ G

Strum ➝ /   /   /   /   /   /   /   /

Count ➝ 1   2   3   4   1   2   3   4

Watch and listen to the video instruction to make sure you're playing correctly. You can access the video by going to this address on the internet:

cvls.com/extras/kidsguitar

G Chord Song

For this course, we're going to use smaller and easier versions of the chords than what most experienced guitarists would play. If you would like to play the full chords, skip to page 42. Now, let's play a song using the G chord.

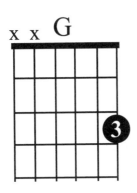

G Chord Song

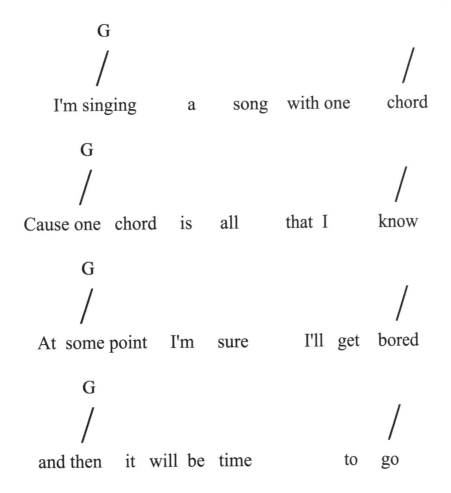

G
/   /
I'm singing   a   song   with one   chord

G
/   /
Cause one   chord   is   all   that I   know

G
/   /
At some point   I'm   sure   I'll get bored

G
/   /
and then   it will be time   to   go

C Chord Song

Let's try a new chord, C. This time we're going to use two fingers to play the chord. We'll place our middle finger on the 2nd fret of the 4th string. Next, we'll place the index finger on the 1st fret of the 2nd string. You can also place your index finger down first and then your middle finger if that's easier for you.

Strum down from the 4th string. Now try playing each string one at a time. Can you hear each note clearly? You may need to arch your fingers more so that they are vertical enough not to touch another string. Also check your finger positions with the frets. Are you in the right spot?

Now play a song using the C chord.

C Chord Song

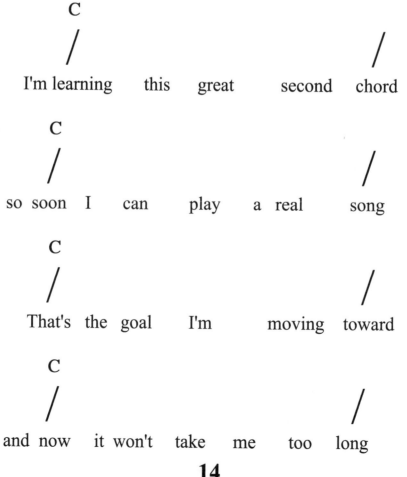

C

/　　　　　　　　　　　/

I'm learning　this　great　second　chord

C

/　　　　　　　　　　　/

so soon　I　can　play　a　real　song

C

/　　　　　　　　　　　/

That's　the　goal　I'm　moving　toward

C

/　　　　　　　　　　　/

and now　it won't　take　me　too　long

14

Changing Chords

We now know how to play two different chords. Before we can start our first real song, we need to work on switching between these chords.

We'll start by using just our left hand and not worry about the right hand. Make a C chord. Now we're going to relax those two fingers and place our ring finger down to make a G. Hold it for a few seconds and then switch back to C.

When you first start learning and switching chords, it's going to take your fingers a little while to get in the correct spot. Over time as you practice, your fingers will start moving to the right positions quicker and quicker.

In our first song, we're going to switch from C to G and back and forth. So try making a C chord, play one strum for a count of (1-2-3-4) and then switching your hands to G and play a strum for a count of 1-2-3-4.

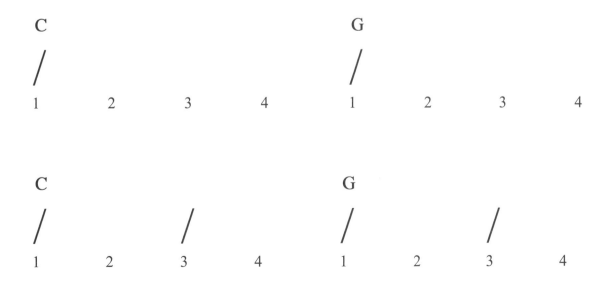

Practice Tips

- Don't try to practice for an hour at a time. Try practicing for ten to twenty minutes once or twice a day.

- Stop if your fingers start to hurt.

- Tune your guitar at the start of each practice session.

- First, watch the video for each song so you can see where your fingers should go and listen to the song.

- Second, practice playing the song with the book as slowly as you need to.

- Once you feel comfortable, try playing along with the video.

- Relax - if you're getting frustrated, try taking a break and coming back to it later. Learning the guitar is supposed to be a fun experience, so enjoy yourself.

- It's ok if you make a mistake while playing a song. You may have to practice the song many times before your fingers remember what to do.

- If some of the notes don't sound right, you may need to arch your fingers more. The more vertical your fingers are, the less likely they are to touch another string.

Section 2
The Songs

He's Got the Whole World 18-19
Mary Had a Little Lamb 20-21
Wheels On the Bus.. 22-23
Row, Row, Row Your Boat 24-25
Hush Little Baby 26-27
Rain, Rain, Go Away... 28-29
Hokey Pokey 30-31
If You're Happy and You Know It............................ 32-33
Itsy Bitsy Spider... 34-35
John Jacob Jingleheimer Schmidt............................ 36-37
Oh When the Saints 38-39
Twinkle Twinkle Little Star 40-41

For Online Video & Audio Access, go to this address on the internet:

cvls.com/extras/kidsguitar

He's Got the Whole World
Chords & Strum

We're ready for our first real song. We're using the C and G chords we just learned and strumming twice per line.

The strum markers match up with the words to the song that you sing at the same time. So for the first line, you would strum while you sing "whole" and then again with "in his".

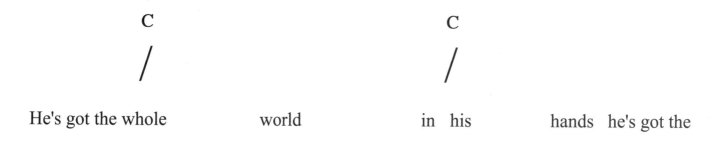

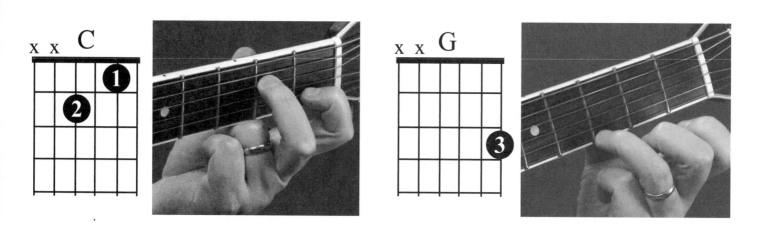

He's Got the Whole World

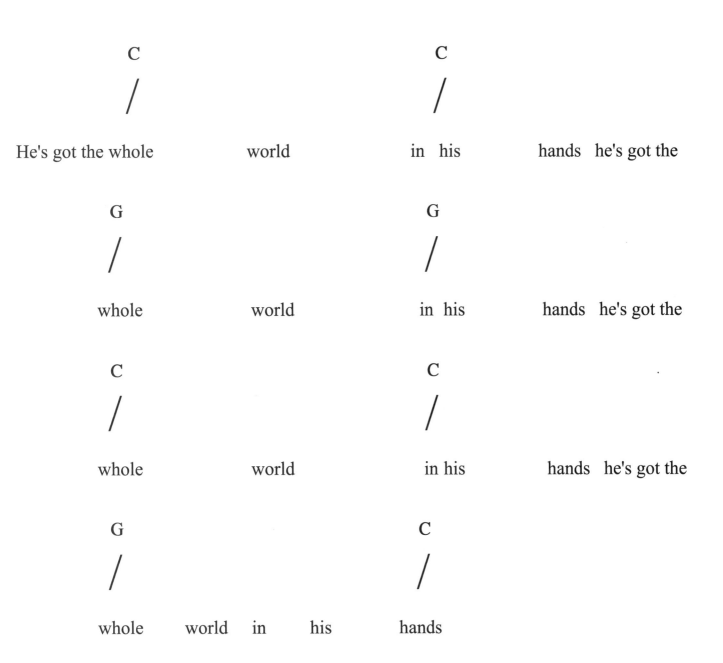

C　　　　　　　　　　C

He's got the whole　　　world　　　in　his　　　hands　he's got the

G　　　　　　　　　　G

whole　　　world　　　in　his　　　hands　he's got the

C　　　　　　　　　　C

whole　　　world　　　in his　　　hands　he's got the

G　　　　　　　　　　C

whole　　world　in　　his　　hands

Watch and listen to the video instruction to make sure you're playing correctly.
You can access the video by going to this address on the internet:

cvls.com/extras/kidsguitar

19

Mary Had a Little Lamb
Chords & Strum

Let's try using the same chords and strum idea with a new song.

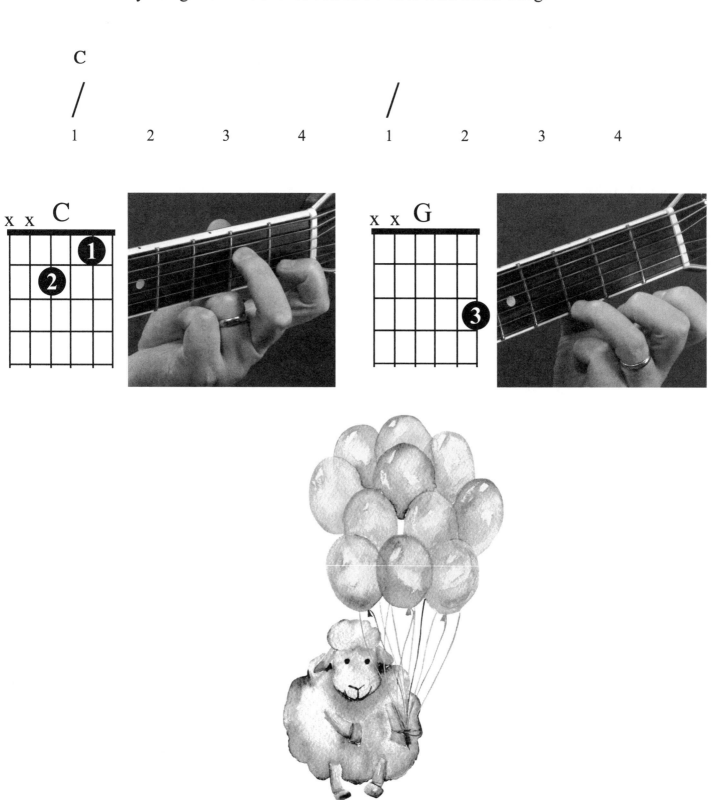

Mary Had a Little Lamb

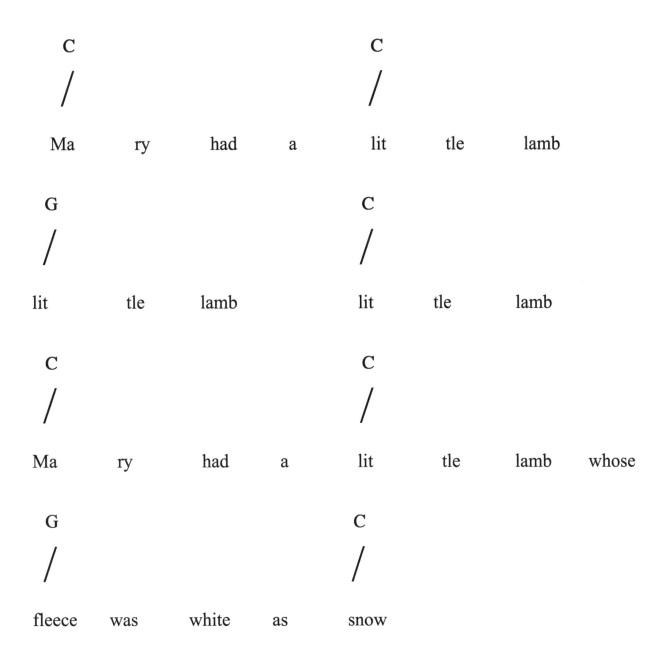

C
/
Ma   ry   had   a

C
/
lit   tle   lamb

G
/
lit   tle   lamb

C
/
lit   tle   lamb

C
/
Ma   ry   had   a

C
/
lit   tle   lamb   whose

G
/
fleece   was   white   as

C
/
snow

Wheels On the Bus
Chords & Strum

We're now going to strum four times for each line of the song.

C

/   /   /   /

1   2   3   4   1   2   3   4

Up to this point, we've shown which chord to play for every strum. Now that we're adding more strums, we'll continue to play the same chord until it changes.

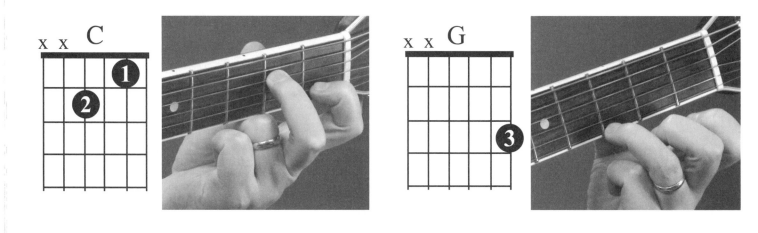

Wheels On the Bus

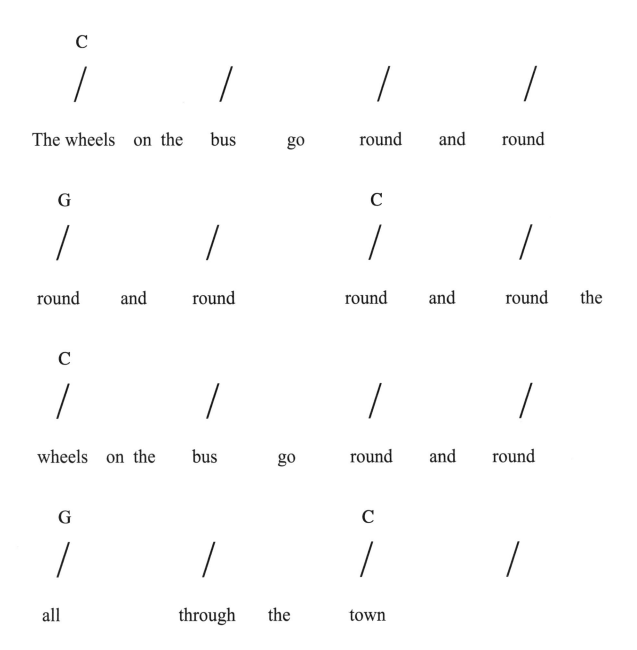

C
/   /   /   /

The wheels on the bus go round and round

G   C
/   /   /   /

round and round round and round the

C
/   /   /   /

wheels on the bus go round and round

G   C
/   /   /   /

all through the town

Row, Row, Row Your Boat
Chords & Strum

For this song, you'll have to switch between the C and G chord a little quicker with your left hand.

C

/   /   /   /

1   2   3   4   1   2   3   4

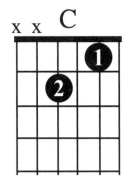

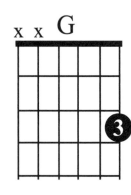

Row, Row, Row Your Boat

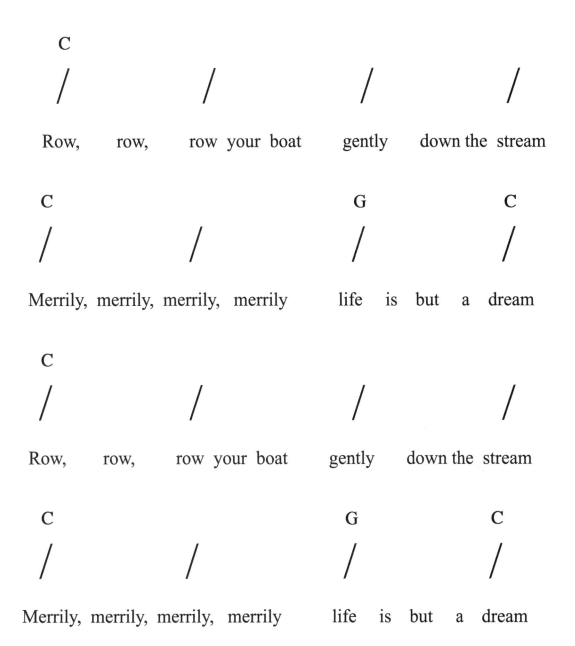

C

/   /   /   /

Row,   row,   row your boat   gently   down the stream

C   G   C

/   /   /   /

Merrily, merrily, merrily, merrily   life   is   but   a   dream

C

/   /   /   /

Row,   row,   row your boat   gently   down the stream

C   G   C

/   /   /   /

Merrily, merrily, merrily, merrily   life   is   but   a   dream

Hush Little Baby
Chords & Strum

It's time to learn a new chord. This chord is called a G⁷. Instead of playing at the 3rd fret like we did with a regular G, we're now playing the 1st fret with our index finger.

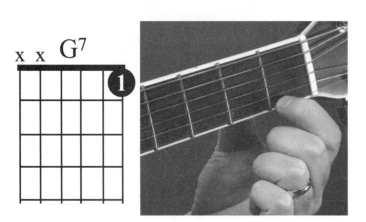 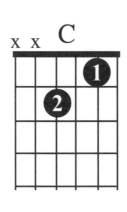 

When you switch between C and G7, you will lift your middle finger up while moving your index finger down one string. Try practicing this switch.

C	G⁷	C	G⁷	C	G⁷	C	G⁷
/	/	/	/	/	/	/	/
1	2	3	4	1	2	3	4

In the song, we'll strum twice per line.

C				G⁷			
/				/			
1	2	3	4	1	2	3	4

Hush Little Baby

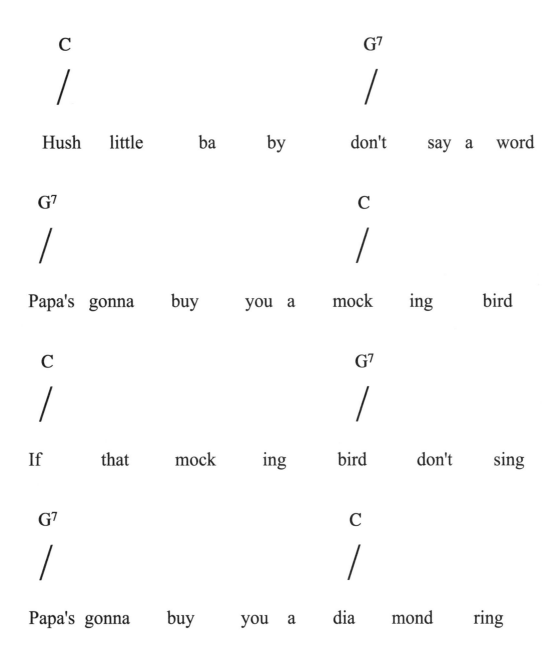

C   G⁷

Hush   little   ba   by   don't   say   a   word

G⁷   C

Papa's   gonna   buy   you   a   mock   ing   bird

C   G⁷

If   that   mock   ing   bird   don't   sing

G⁷   C

Papa's   gonna   buy   you   a   dia   mond   ring

Rain, Rain, Go Away
Chords & Strum

Let's use C and G7 again in a new song. This time we'll play four strums per line.

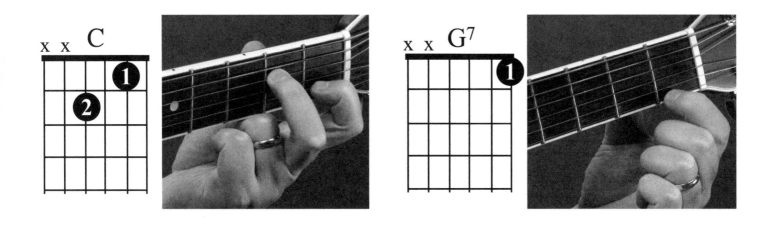

C

/ / / /

1   2   3   4   1   2   3   4

Rain, Rain, Go Away

C

/   /   /   /

Rain,   rain,   go   a   way

C

/   /   /   /

come   a   gain   some   o   ther   day

G⁷

/   /   /   /

Lit   tle   chil   dren   want   to   play

G⁷   **C**

/   /   /   /

rain,   rain,   go   a   way

Hokey Pokey
Chords & Strum

We'll play four strums per line with the C and G7 chords.

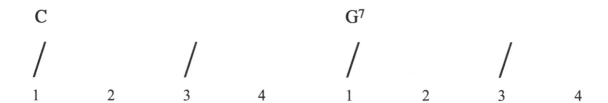

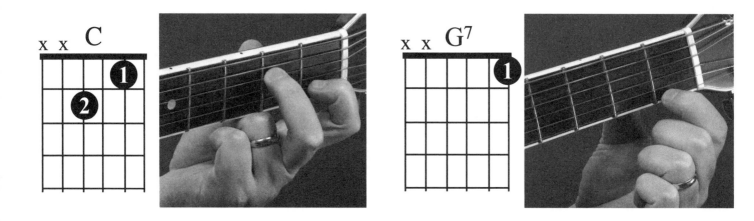

Hokey Pokey

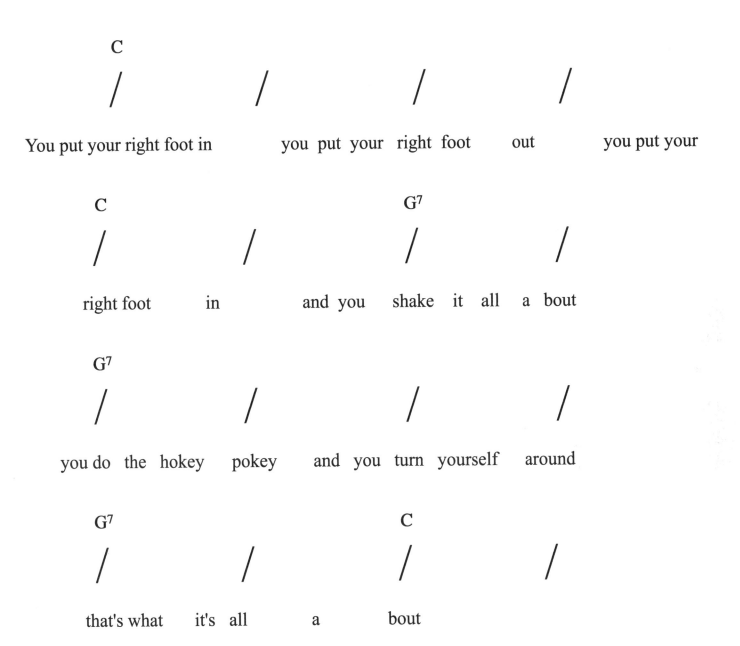

C
/   /   /   /

You put your right foot in   you put your right foot   out   you put your

C   G⁷
/   /   /   /

right foot   in   and you   shake it all a bout

G⁷
/   /   /   /

you do the hokey pokey   and you turn yourself   around

G⁷   C
/   /   /   /

that's what   it's all   a   bout

If You're Happy and You Know It
Chords & Strum

It's time to learn a new chord. The D chord uses three fingers.

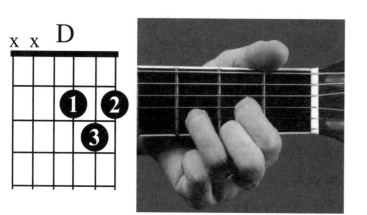
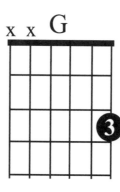

Practice playing each string, one at a time. Is each note clear? Or do you hear a buzz or soft note? You may need to arch your fingers more to get a clear sound. Once you can play it clearly, practice switching between the G and D chords.

G	D	G	D	G	D	G	D
/	/	/	/	/	/	/	/
1	2	3	4	1	2	3	4

We'll play two strums per line for this song.

G				D			
/				/			
1	2	3	4	1	2	3	4

D				G			
/		/		/		/	
1	2	3	4	1	2	3	4

If You're Happy and You Know It

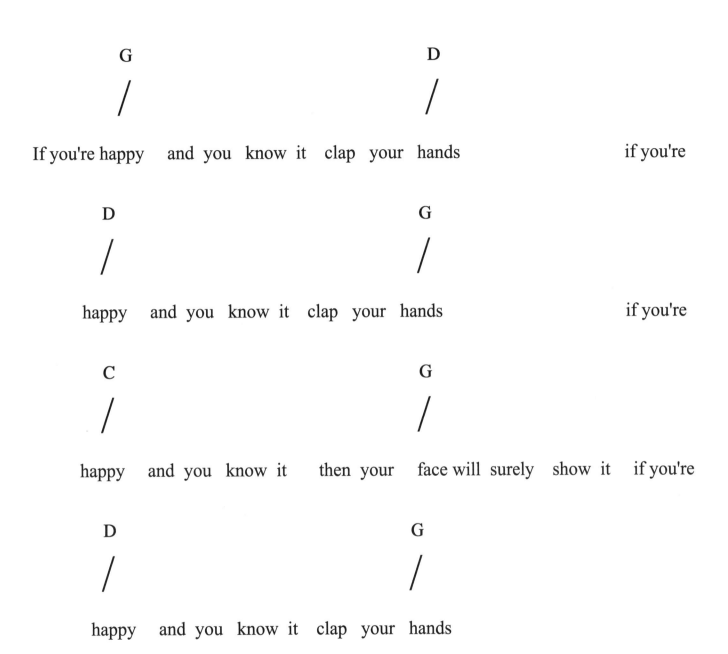

G   /   D   /

If you're happy   and you know it clap your hands   if you're

D   /   G   /

happy   and you know it clap your hands   if you're

C   /   G   /

happy   and you know it then your face will surely show it if you're

D   /   G   /

happy   and you know it clap your hands

Itsy Bitsy Spider
Chords & Strum

We'll strum four times per line in the next song. The chord changes chords will be a bit faster so you may need to practice this very slowly.

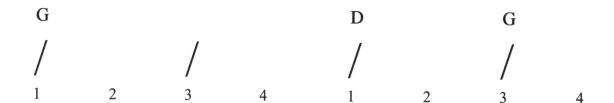

Let's use the G, C, and D chords again in this song.

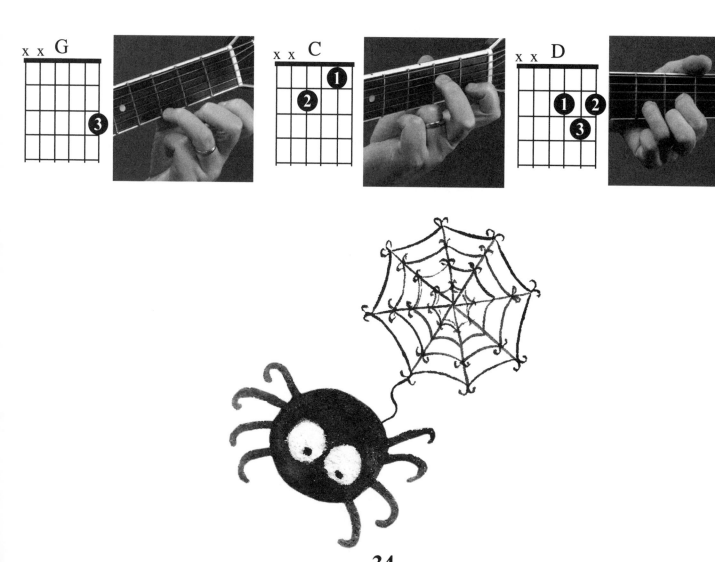

Itsy Bitsy Spider

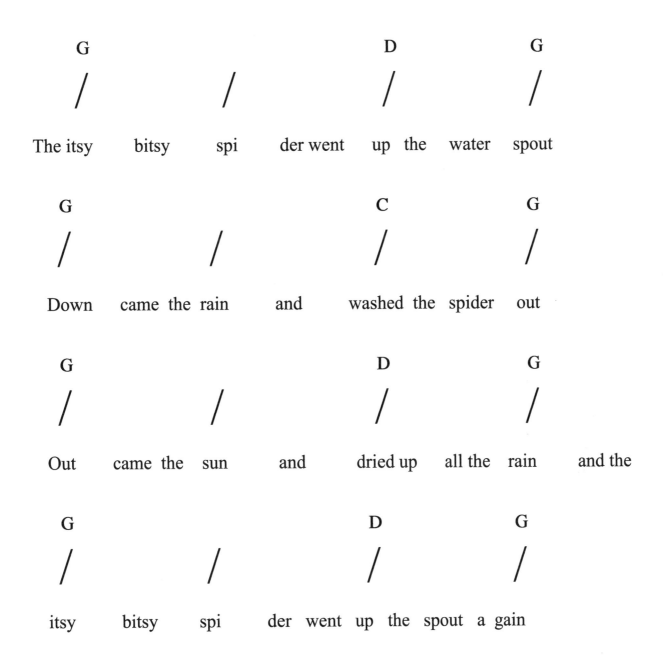

G /   /   D /   G /

The itsy   bitsy   spi   der went   up   the   water   spout

G /   /   C /   G /

Down   came the rain   and   washed the spider   out

G /   /   D /   G /

Out   came the sun   and   dried up   all the   rain   and the

G /   /   D /   G /

itsy   bitsy   spi   der went up the spout a gain

John Jacob Jingleheimer Schmidt
Chords & Strum

We're going to use the same three chords, G, C, and D, but this is the first time we switch from C to D. Let's practice that.

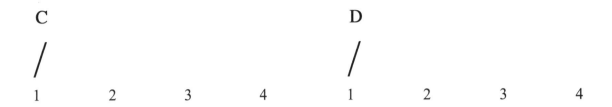

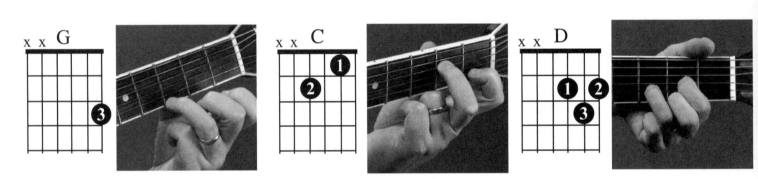

We'll strum down four times per line for the next song.

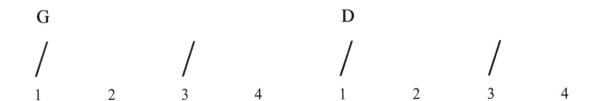

John Jacob Jingleheimer Schmidt

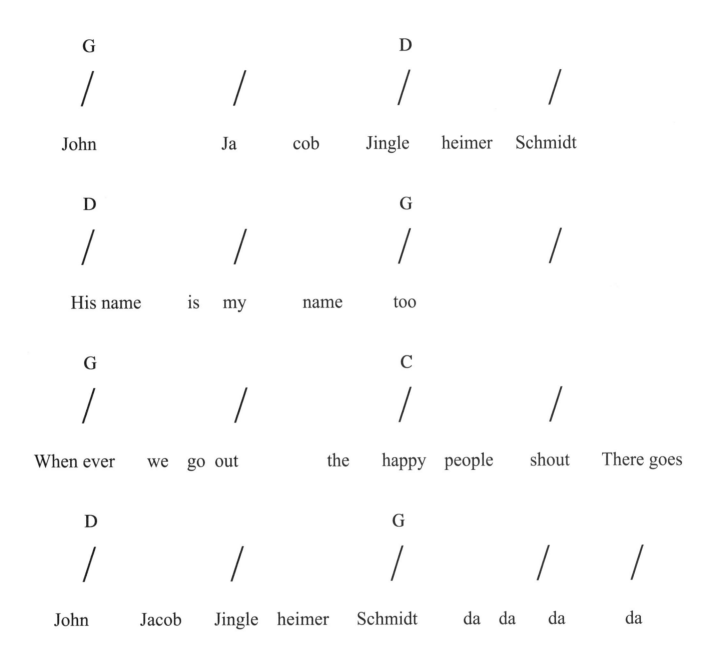

Oh When the Saints
Chords & Strum

We'll strum four times per line in the next song.

G

/   /   /   /

1   2   3   4   1   2   3   4

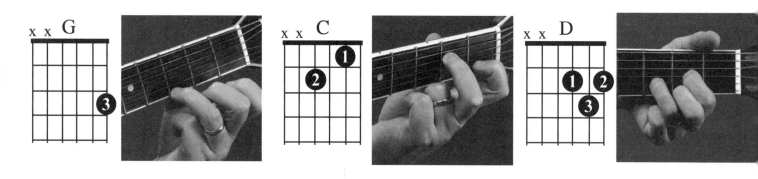

Oh When the Saints

G
/   /   /   /

Oh when the Saints   go   march   ing

G
/   /   /   /

in   oh   when   the

G
/   /   /   /

Saints   go   march   ing

D
/   /   /   /

in   Oh   how   I

G
/   /   /   /

want   to   be   in   that

C
/   /   /   /

num   ber   Oh   when   the

G   D
/   /   /   /

Saints   go   march   ing

G
/   /   /   /

in

Twinkle Twinkle Little Star
Chords & Strum

We'll strum eight times per line in the next song.

G   C   G

/   /   /   /   /   /   /   /

1   2   3   4   1   2   3   4

Once again, we'll use the G, C, and D chords.

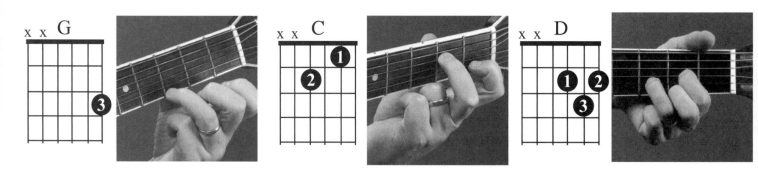

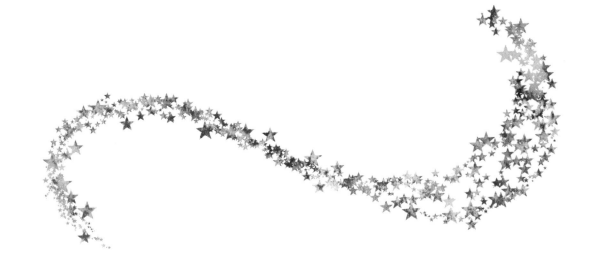

Twinkle Twinkle Little Star

G				C		G	
/	/	/	/	/	/	/	/
Twin	kle	twin	kle	lit	tle	star	

C		G		D		G	
/	/	/	/	/	/	/	/
how	I	won	der	what	you	are	

G		C		G		D	
/	/	/	/	/	/	/	/
high	a	bove	the	world	so	high	

G		C		G		D	
/	/	/	/	/	/	/	/
like	a	dia	mond	in	the	sky	

G				C		G	
/	/	/	/	/	/	/	/
Twin	kle	twin	kle	lit	tle	star	

C		G		D		G	
/	/	/	/	/	/	/	/
how	I	won	der	what	you	are	

Section 3
The Songs with Full Chords

Note: Section 3 is a duplicate of Section 2, but using full chords instead of the beginner chords that we started with. These are the chords that most guitar players use when they get past the absolute beginner stage.

He's Got the Whole World 44-45

Mary Had a Little Lamb 46-47

Wheels On the Bus.. 48-49

Row, Row, Row Your Boat 50-51

Hush Little Baby 52-53

Rain, Rain, Go Away... 54-55

Hokey Pokey 56-57

If You're Happy and You Know It............................... 58-59

Itsy Bitsy Spider.. 60-61

John Jacob Jingleheimer Schmidt............................. 62-63

Oh When the Saints 64-65

Twinkle Twinkle Little Star 66-67

Common Chords 68-69

Other Products 70-71

Full Chords

The chords below are a little bit harder to play. You will need to use proper thumb placement like we discussed in Section 1 of this course. If you don't hear each note clearly, make sure your finger are arched and close to vertical. This will help prevent them from getting in the way of another string.

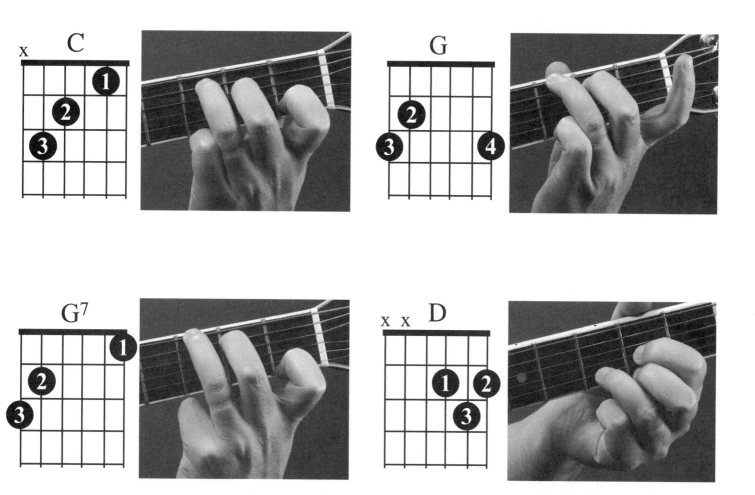

He's Got the Whole World
Chords & Strum

We're ready for our first song. We're using the C and G chords we just learned and strumming twice per line.

C   G

/   /

1   2   3   4   1   2   3   4

The strum markers match up with the words to the song that you sing at the same time. So for the first line, you would strum while you sing "whole" and then again with "in his".

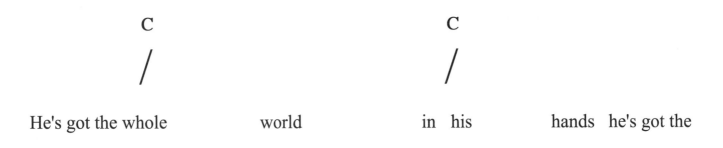

C   C

/   /

He's got the whole   world   in his   hands he's got the

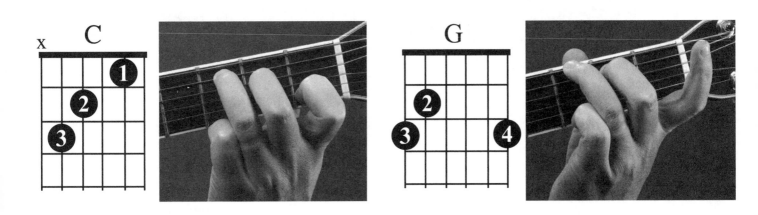

44

He's Got the Whole World

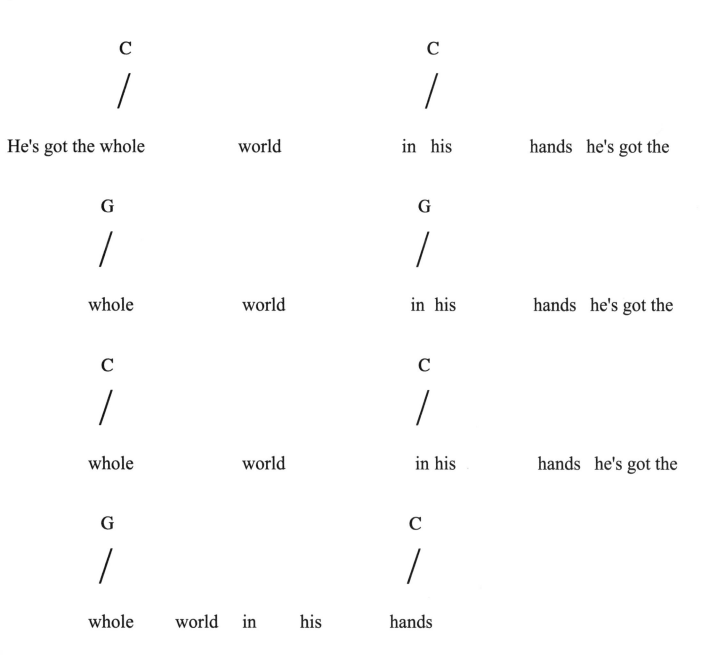

C   C

He's got the whole   world   in his   hands   he's got the

G   G

whole   world   in his   hands   he's got the

C   C

whole   world   in his   hands   he's got the

G   C

whole   world   in   his   hands

Mary Had a Little Lamb
Chords & Strum

Let's try using the same chords and strum idea with another song.

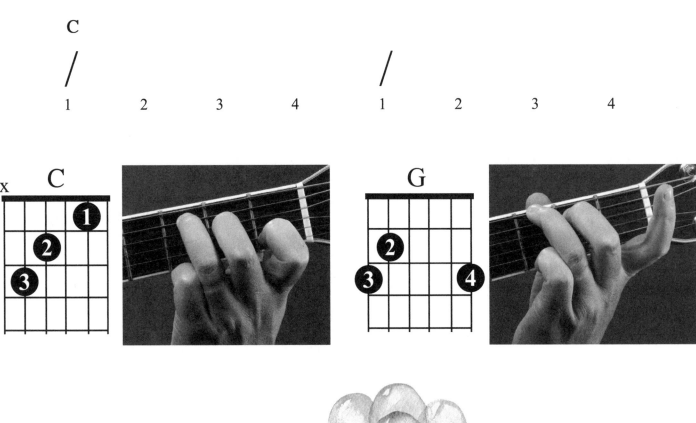

Mary Had a Little Lamb

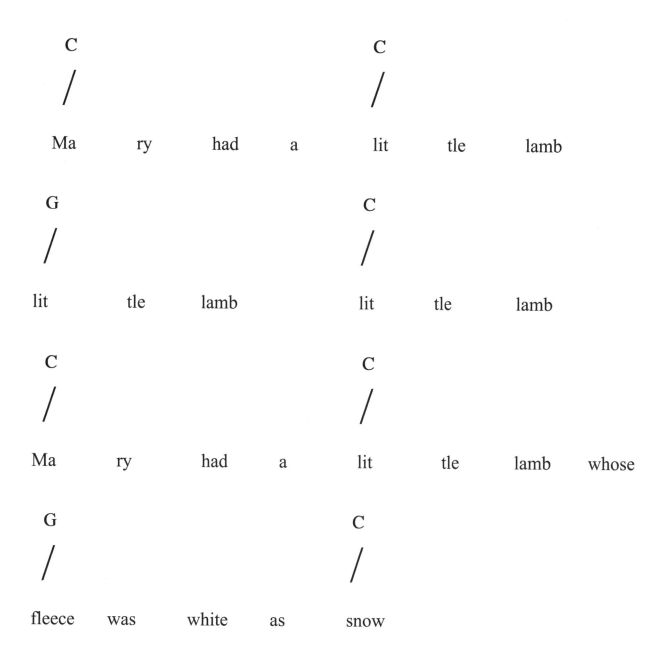

C

/

Ma   ry   had   a   lit   tle   lamb

C

/

G

/

lit   tle   lamb

C

/

lit   tle   lamb

C

/

Ma   ry   had   a   lit   tle   lamb   whose

C

/

G

/

fleece   was   white   as   snow

C

/

Wheels On the Bus
Chords & Strum

We're now going to strum four times for each line of the song.

C

/		/		/		/	
1	2	3	4	1	2	3	4

Up to this point, we've shown which chord to play for every strum. Now that we're adding more strums, we'll continue to play the same chord until it changes.

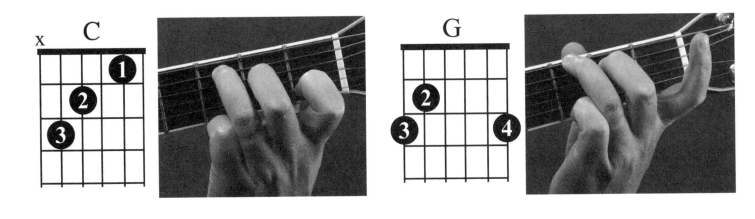

Wheels On the Bus

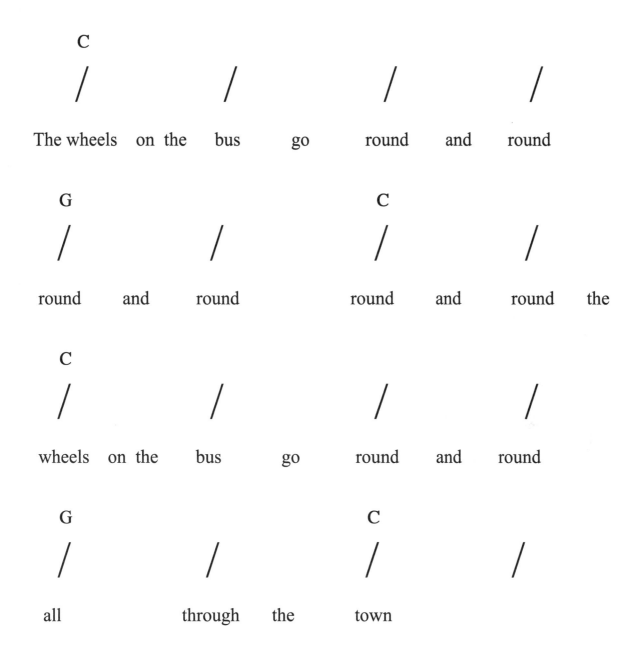

C
/   /   /   /

The wheels on the bus go round and round

G   C
/   /   /   /

round and round round and round the

C
/   /   /   /

wheels on the bus go round and round

G   C
/   /   /   /

all through the town

Row, Row, Row Your Boat
Chords & Strum

For this song, you'll have to switch between the C and G chord a little quicker with your left hand.

C

/   /   /   /
1   2   3   4   1   2   3   4

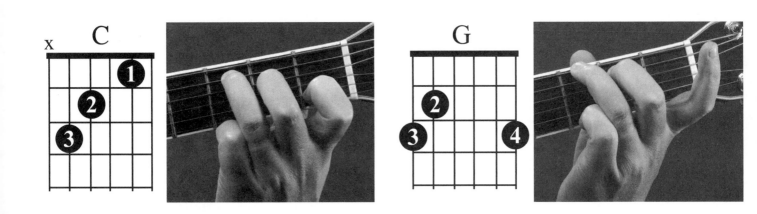

Row, Row, Row Your Boat

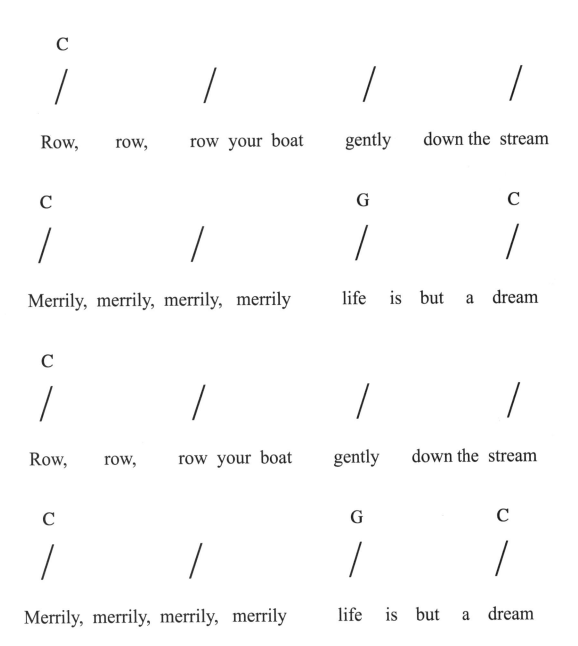

Hush Little Baby
Chords & Strum

It's time to learn a new chord. This chord is called a G^7. Instead of playing at the 3rd fret like we did with a regular G, we're now playing the 1st fret with our index finger.

G^7

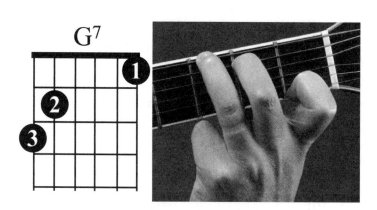

x C

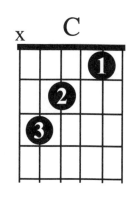

Try practicing this switch.

C	G^7	C	G^7	C	G^7	C	G^7
/	/	/	/	/	/	/	/
1	2	3	4	1	2	3	4

In the song, we'll strum twice per line.

C				G^7			
/				/			
1	2	3	4	1	2	3	4

Hush Little Baby

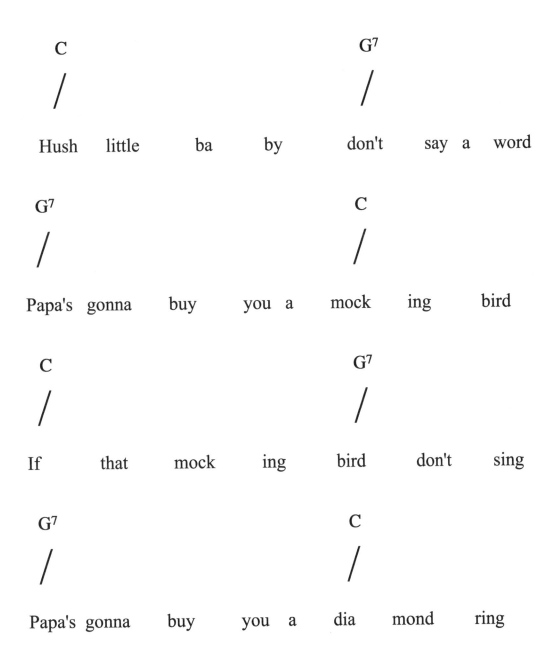

C　　　　　　　　　　　　　G⁷

Hush　　little　　ba　　by　　don't　　say　a　word

G⁷　　　　　　　　　　　C

Papa's　gonna　buy　　you　a　mock　ing　bird

C　　　　　　　　　　　　　G⁷

If　　that　　mock　ing　bird　don't　sing

G⁷　　　　　　　　　　　C

Papa's　gonna　buy　　you　a　dia　mond　ring

Rain, Rain, Go Away
Chords & Strum

Let's use C and G7 again in another song. This time we'll play four strums per line.

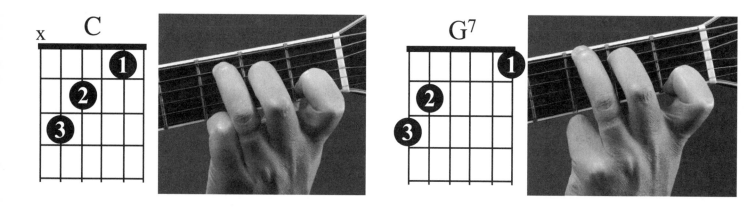

C

/   /   /   /

1   2   3   4   1   2   3   4

Rain, Rain, Go Away

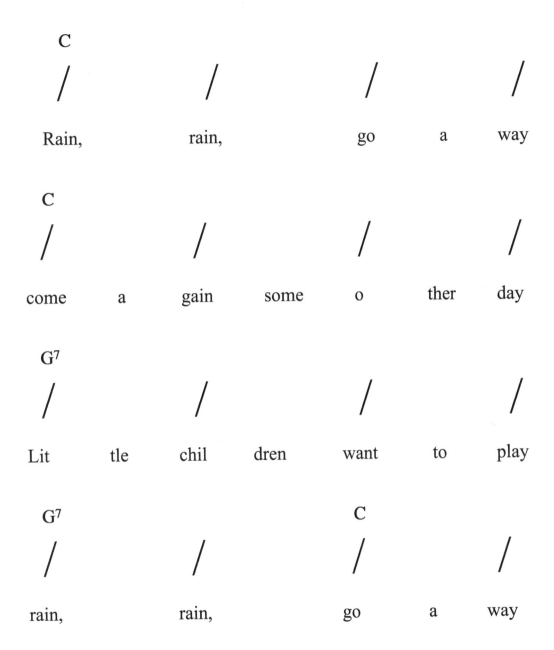

C
/   /   /   /

Rain,   rain,   go   a   way

C
/   /   /   /

come   a   gain   some   o   ther   day

G⁷
/   /   /   /

Lit   tle   chil   dren   want   to   play

G⁷   C
/   /   /   /

rain,   rain,   go   a   way

Hokey Pokey
Chords & Strum

We'll play four strums per line with the C and G7 chords.

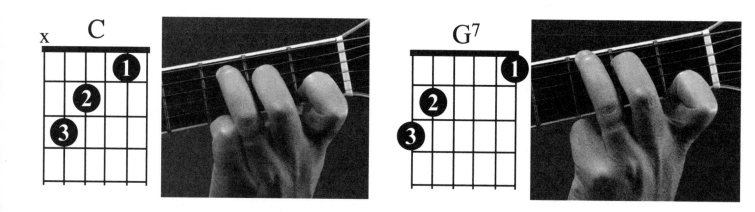

Hokey Pokey

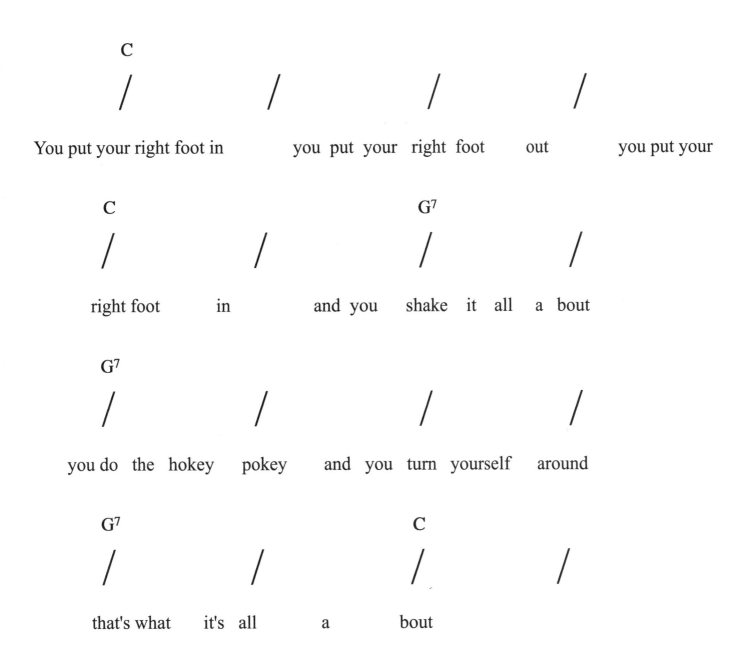

C

/   /   /   /

You put your right foot in   you put your right foot   out   you put your

C   G⁷

/   /   /   /

right foot   in   and you   shake it all a bout

G⁷

/   /   /   /

you do the hokey   pokey   and you turn yourself   around

G⁷   C

/   /   /   /

that's what   it's all   a   bout

If You're Happy and You Know It
Chords & Strum

The D chord is the same as the beginner version. You don't have to learn a new D chord.

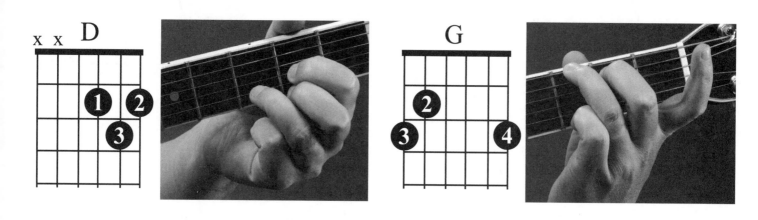

Practice playing each string, one at a time. Is each note clear? Or do you hear a buzz or soft note? You may need to arch your fingers more to get a clear sound. Once you can play it clearly, practice switching between the G and D chords.

G	D	G	D	G	D	G	D
/	/	/	/	/	/	/	/
1	2	3	4	1	2	3	4

We'll play two strums per line for this song.

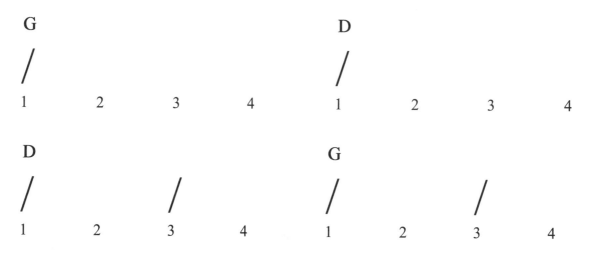

If You're Happy and You Know It

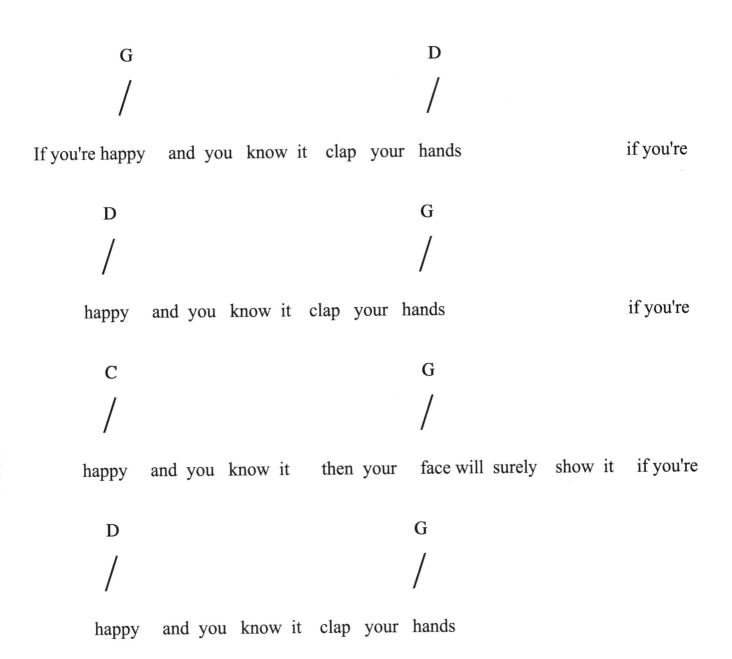

G   D

If you're happy   and you know it clap your hands   if you're

D   G

happy   and you know it clap your hands   if you're

C   G

happy   and you know it   then your   face will surely show it   if you're

D   G

happy   and you know it clap your hands

Itsy Bitsy Spider
Chords & Strum

We'll strum four times per line in the next song. The chord changes chords will be a bit faster so you may need to practice this very slowly.

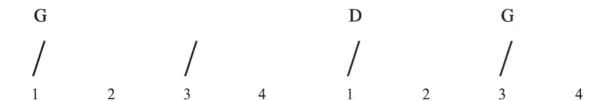

Let's use the G, C, and D chords again in this song.

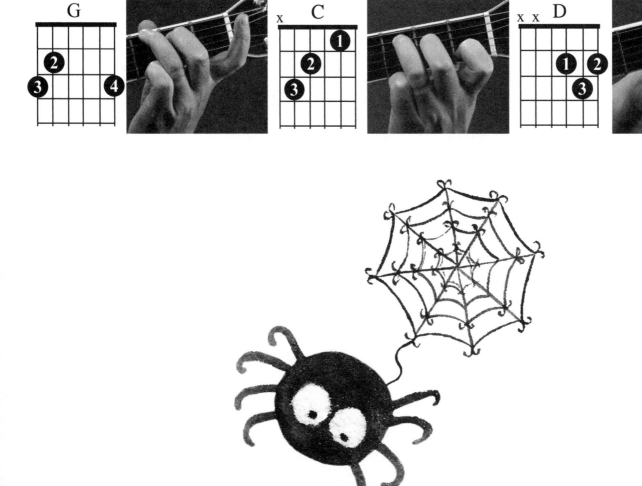

Itsy Bitsy Spider

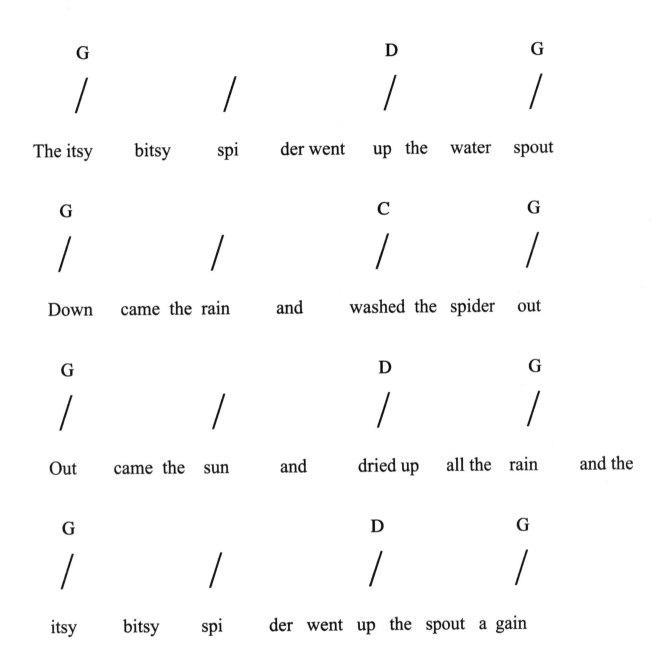

G / / D / G /

The itsy bitsy spi der went up the water spout

G / / C / G /

Down came the rain and washed the spider out

G / / D / G /

Out came the sun and dried up all the rain and the

G / / D / G /

itsy bitsy spi der went up the spout a gain

John Jacob Jingleheimer Schmidt
Chords & Strum

We're going to use the same three chords, G, C, and D, but this is the first time we switch from C to D. Let's practice that.

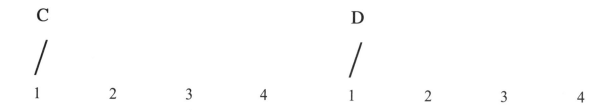

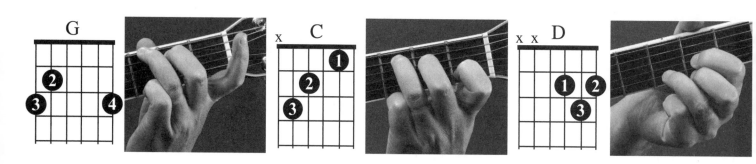

We'll strum down four times per line for the next song.

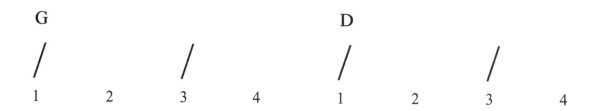

John Jacob Jingleheimer Schmidt

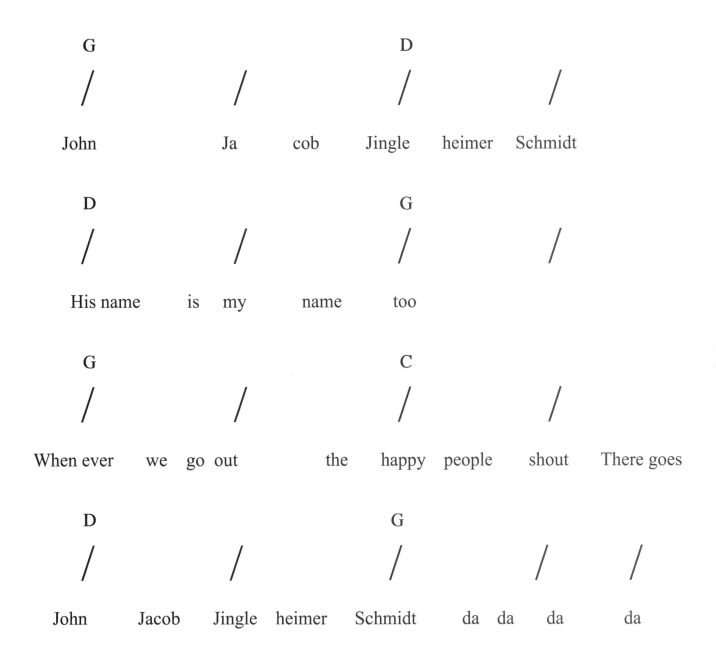

Oh When the Saints
Chords & Strum

We'll strum four times per line in the next song.

G

/   /   /   /

1   2   3   4   1   2   3   4

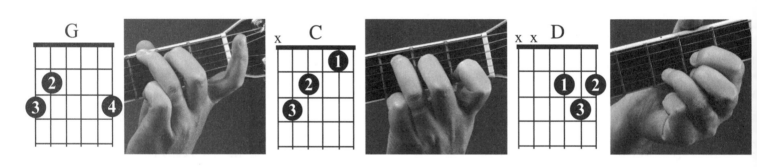

Oh When the Saints

G
/   /   /   /

Oh when the Saints   go   march   ing

G
/   /   /   /

in   oh   when   the

G
/   /   /   /

Saints   go   march   ing

D
/   /   /   /

in   Oh   how   I

G
/   /   /   /

want   to   be   in   that

C
/   /   /   /

num   ber   Oh   when   the

G   D
/   /   /   /

Saints   go   march   ing

G
/   /   /   /

in

Twinkle Twinkle Little Star
Chords & Strum

We'll strum eight times per line in the next song.

G   C   G

/   /   /   /   /   /   /   /

1   2   3   4   1   2   3   4

Once again, we'll use the G, C, and D chords.

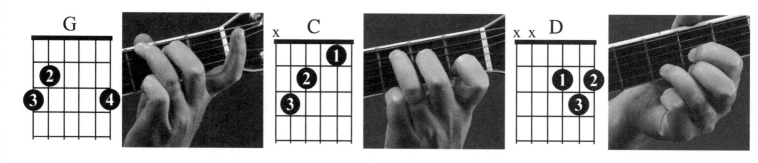

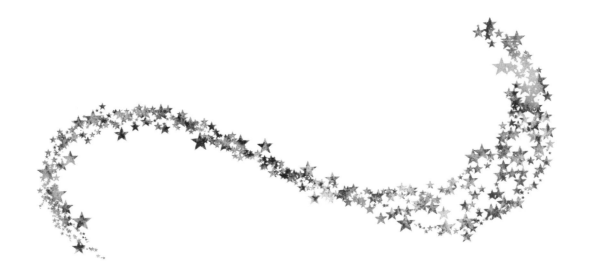

Twinkle Twinkle Little Star

G / / / **C** / **G** / /
Twin kle twin kle lit tle star

C / **G** / **D** / **G** /
how I won der what you are

G / **C** / **G** / **D** /
high a bove the world so high

G / **C** / **G** / **D** /
like a dia mond in the sky

G / / / **C** / **G** / /
Twin kle twin kle lit tle star

C / **G** / **D** / **G** /
how I won der what you are

Common Chords

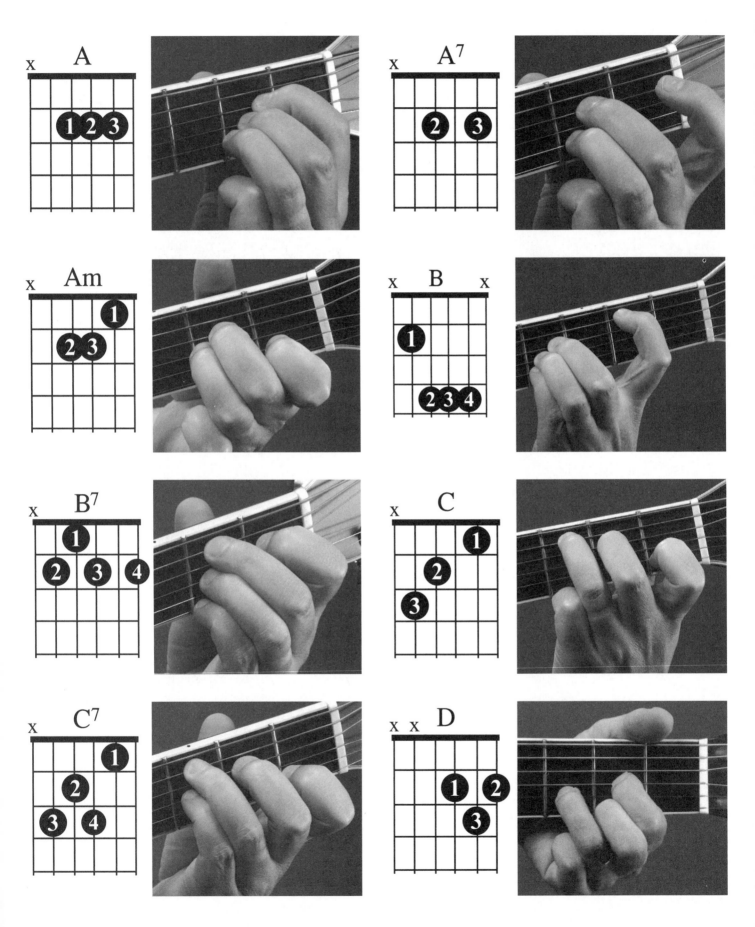

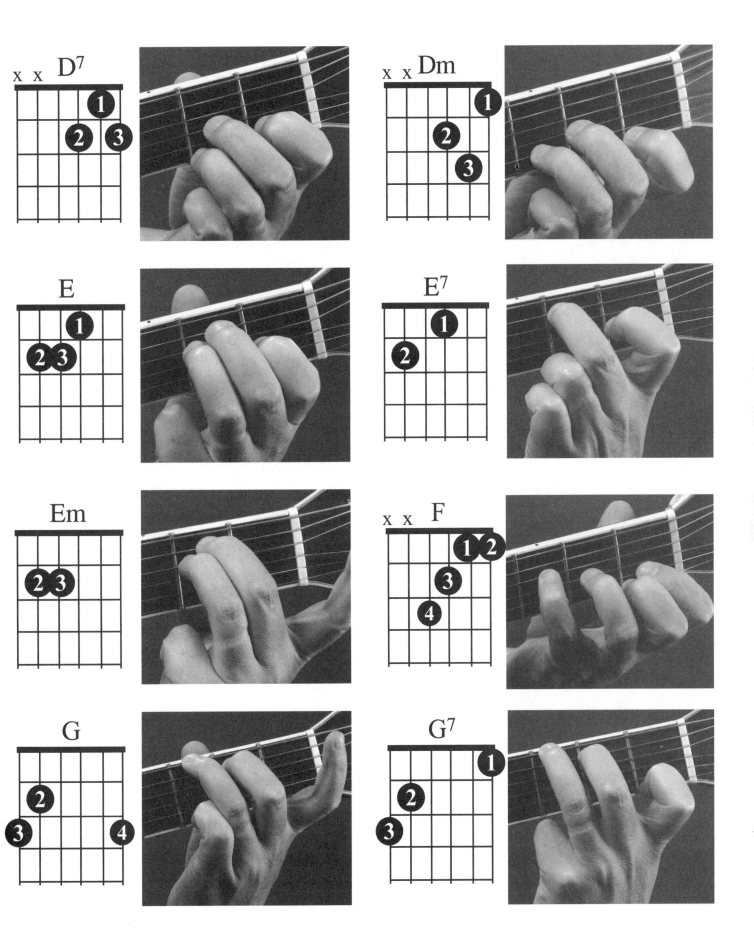

69

Beginner Series for Kids

Watch & Learn, Inc. has other products for elementary school-aged children. These can be used with this course or on its own.

Designed to quickly teach the beginning student to play songs they will know and love. These lessons start by playing with just the right hand and gradually build to adding the left hand thumb and learning how to play with both hands. Song arrangements provide an easy transition from learning the basics to covering more interesting rhythms, techniques, and musical ideas. The book features standard music notation for each song and exercise along with fingering notation and hand shifts to make the course easier to learn. This method includes online access to over an hour of video instruction that will help the child play with proper form and timing. The combination of book, video, and audio make this the easiest to understand piano course for kids available.

Designed to help the absolute beginning student learn to play the ukulele. This step-by-step course is designed for elementary school-aged children (ages 5-10) and quickly teaches the student to play songs they will know and love. These lessons teach beginner chords (C, G, G7, F) that are easier for younger students with smaller hands. Song arrangements and strum patterns were carefully selected to help children have early success playing the ukulele. This course will help the young beginner avoid getting frustrated and quitting the instrument.

This beginner method includes online access to video instruction and audio tracks. The video lessons allow the child to hear and see how each song is played from a rhythm and technique standpoint. The video also shows the ukulele, both hands, and the sheet music on-screen at the same time.

Follow-up Products

These Watch & Learn products are also available and would be the next step beyond this course.

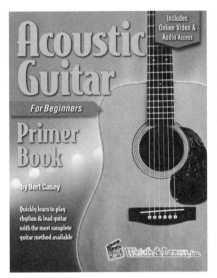

The student starts off by learning beginning concepts like parts of the guitar, proper playing position, strumming, chords, and how to read guitar tabs. Later, you will learn how to play easy songs and then more advanced techniques. The course includes a complete chord chart, an hour of video instruction, and all music is written in both standard music notation and tablature with lyrics and melody lines. This beginner method contains 18 songs that are demonstrated at three speeds each along with an acoustic band, including vocals. This course is suited for beginners ranging from kids to adults.

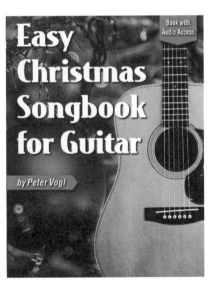

Features beginner to intermediate arrangements for classic Christmas songs. Each song features detailed strum patterns, chord charts, lyrics, and vocal melody notation. The songs were arranged so that you can play the rhythm guitar part while singing along. The second portion of this book displays each song along with extended lyrics and chord progressions. This is a great setup for sing-alongs because the lyrics are written in a large font so that multiple singers and musicians can read along. This course also includes online access to audio tracks to help you learn and practice.

All of these products are available at Amazon.com.